"My mission in life is not merely to survive,
but to thrive; and to do so with some passion,
some compassion, some humor, and some style."
- Maya Angelo

This book is dedicated to endless possibility and productive positivity.

# TABLE OF CONTENTS

# FORWARD

## ABOUT THIS PROGRAM

Thank you for your interest in this program! This book is a preview of the multiple tools available in **The Enlightened Diva Collection** - a stylishly designed toolkit to have you focused and feeling like a boss. Why is the program split into parts?

First, I don't want you to feel overwhelmed. **The program is designed to be incredibly introspective and promote significant insight** into:

(a) your mindset,

(b) the difference between your current vs. idealized lifestyle,

(c) identifying and realistically defining your goals,

(d) redefining and aligning your current priorities with your goal, and

(e) confronting/accepting the obstacles and consequences of your decisions.

In other words, fully participating and significantly benefitting from this program requires a lot from you and covers a lot of ground. It can be challenging to fully admit and confront the both realities of your situation and the sacrifices involved for you to fully focus on pursuing your goals. Be particularly kind and open to fully embracing your personal growth journey.

Second, I don't want for you to feel like this purchase was a waste of time and money. Accordingly, I've published this shortened 3-Day Preview to reduce printing costs and pass the savings on to you! This way, if this program doesn't benefit you, we've limited your investment.

Third, I've designed this program to maximize your chances of meeting your goal. The purpose here is to simplify your target to one aspect of a personal problem so that you can achieve a win or significant progress relatively easily. You'll benefit from improved well-being and gain a critical confidence boost to build on.

**//** Success is not the key to happiness. Happiness is the key to success.

- Albert Schweitzer

**SPIT FIRE:** Celebrate and contemplate how your personal growth journey affects use. I'm particularly inspired by words; so, I use poetry modeled off the the rhythm, excitement, and confidence of rap/hip-hop verses or flows;

**INSPIRE:** Utilize popular spiritual and wellness practices/tools to encourage a deeply authentic and clearer insight into your life so that you can identify the elements/features of your idealized life.

**SOAR HIGHER:** Utilize proven psychological and success techniques/tools to better understand yourself so that you can develop a customized strategy to realize your goals.

**Cognitive Behavioral Therapy (CBT) |** psychological treatment/intervention tool that has been demonstrated to be effective for a range of problems including mental issues like depression and anxiety.

**Color Therapy |** Color is a powerful communication tool that's believed to influence mood, actions, and physiological reaction (e.g. increased blood pressure). The program selects some colors with particularly powerful associations. We also provide a swatch of each color for you to place wherever you want to be inspired and reminded about your program goals.

**Life Coaching |** A service that helps you improve your daily life and well-being by helping you: 1) identify/clarify your priorities and goals; and 2) develop strategies to identify/overcome issues and obstacles.

**Life Planning |** Creating a flexible framework that helps you identify priorities, make good decisions, and increase positivity and well-being. There's also an optional Life Planner in the Appendix to use if you don't already have a good system in place.

**Positive Psychology Interventions (PPIs) |** tools and strategies with demonstrated success that focus on increasing positivity, happiness, and wellbeing.

**Spirituality |** Health-related behaviors that seek/ promote by personal growth/reflection, creativity, and emotional maturation. The program utilizes tarot to promote reflection, insight, and strategizing to reach your goals.

# FIRST STEPS

**Step 1 |** Check whether you're likely to benefit from this program by completing this chapter. If you score highly or have minimal issues/concerns, you may not significantly benefit from this program. Nevertheless, you may enjoy completing the program as a means to capture your current progress on your personal journey. Skip ahead to the Life Satisfaction and Personal Growth Ambition Check to see how highly you score.

**Step 2 |** Gather your supplies. You may want to keep these close by during the day. You can also have a supply set at your usual locations during your mood tracker times in particular.

☐ Gather Supplies

    ☐ Coloring Supplies (e.g. colored pencils)

    ☐ Scissors

    ☐ Tape or Glue

    ☐ Pen or Pencil For Writing

    ☐ Diva Collection Tarot Cards (Purchase In-Store, Online, or Create a Quick Set Using the Tarot Card Images in the Appendix). If you choose to make your own tarot set from this book. Carefully remove the pages from this book and time away the excess white space.

Then, simply glue or tape the front and backs. Pro-Tip: I've left the back of the card pages blank so that your final result is thicker. However, you can use a thicker paper like card-stock between the layers if you'd like to make a more luxe set.

☐ Set Times for Mood Trackers

☐ Fill in the Calendar to Cover the Dates of your 30-day Program.

**Step 3 |** Decide whether you'd like to continue using the program. For your next purchase, you can either purchase the book with days 4 - 30. Or, you can buy the complete program and simply copy or re-write your responses for the first 3 days. I've included the program overview to help you assess your interest.

Thank you so much for your interest and I sincerely hope that **ABSOLUTELY LOVE** this program and that it benefits you as much as it has me! I'd love to get your feedback when it's time to revise this edition. Email me at naci@relgis.llc or message me via the site where your completed your purchase.

Respectfully,

Naci Sigler

## LIFE SATISFACTION

Instructions: Below are five statements that you may agree or disagree with. Using the 1 - 7 scale below, indicate your agreement with each item by placing the appropriate number on the line preceding that item. Please be open and honest in your responding.

> 7 - Strongly agree
>
> 6 - Agree
>
> 5 - Slightly agree
>
> 4 - Neither agree nor disagree
>
> 3 - Slightly disagree
>
> 2 - Disagree
>
> 1 - Strongly disagree

_____ In most ways my life is close to my ideal.

_____ The conditions of my life are excellent.

_____ I am satisfied with my life.

_____ So far I have gotten the important things I want in life.

_____ If I could live my life over, I would change almost nothing.

_____ Total [Enter Total in Score Tracker]

* If your score 30 - 35, you may not see significant gains from this program. Skip ahead to the Pre-Journey Personal Growth Ambition Check to see if you'll benefit from this program.

## THE WORST PIECES OF ME...

*Mark 3 - 5 of your negative traits.*

| | | |
|---|---|---|
| ADDICTED | GRUMPY | PARANOID |
| ANTISOCIAL | HOSTILE | POSSESSIVE |
| CHILDISH | HYPOCRITICAL | PREJUDICED |
| CONTROLLING | IMPATIENT | SELF-DESTRUCTIVE |
| COWARDLY | IMPULSIVE | SELFISH |
| CRUEL | INSECURE | SPOILED |
| CYNICAL | IRRESPONSIBLE | STUBBORN |
| DEFENSIVE | JEALOUS | STUPID |
| DISHONEST | JUDGMENTAL | UGLY |
| DISLOYAL | LAZY | UNGRATEFUL |
| DISORGANIZED | MANIPULATIVE | VAIN |
| DISRESPECTFUL | MATERIALISTIC | VINDICTIVE |
| EVIL | NAGGING | VIOLENT |
| FLAKY | NEEDY | WITHDRAWN |
| FOOLISH | NERVOUS | WORKAHOLIC |
| GREEDY | NOSY | WORRYWART |

SELF-DEVELOPMENT &
LEARNING

RELATIONSHIPS

CAREER & FINANCES

HEALTH & WELLNESS

## Who or What Am I Called to Be?

Write a few words about what your best self calls
you to be in each of these areas. Then, use a
different color to write how you are currently.

Are you having any physical symptoms that you think may be connected to stress or other mental concerns?

_____

_____

_____

...........................................................................................................

**List some of the problems/issues you have in each area.**

**Work/School/Professional Obligations:**

_____

_____

_____

Family Issues/Problems:

_____

_____

_____

Friends:

_____

_____

_____

Other Area: _____

_____

_____

_____

Other Area: _____

_____

_____

_____

_____

## Why did you choose this book?

I initially noticed and was attracted to this book by/since it…

_____

_____

### Initial Goal:

What's one of your current goals that you could accomplish in the next 30 days?

_____

_____

**[Copy this to the Part 1 Log Page in the Appendix]**

# MY REALMS: IDENTIFYING & SELECTING YOUR PERSONAL PROGRAM PRIORITY

In order for you to get the most out of this program, it's vital that you identify your priorities or what you value most in life since performing well in that area will make you feel particularly capable, empowered and satisfied.

To help find your path, start by determining your priorities. Rank the areas of your life on the scales below on a scale of -3 (not important at all) to +3 (very important). Then, write the ranking in the space beside the area. You may specify other areas at the end of the activity.

**Friendships | Rating: _____**

| -3 | -2 | -1 | -0 | 1 | 2 | 3 |
|---|---|---|---|---|---|---|

**Family Life | Rating: _____**

| -3 | -2 | -1 | -0 | 1 | 2 | 3 |
|---|---|---|---|---|---|---|

**Health | Rating: _____**

| -3 | -2 | -1 | -0 | 1 | 2 | 3 |
|---|---|---|---|---|---|---|

Professional Life (e.g. school, work, organization) | Rating: _____

-3          -2          -1          -0          1          2          3

Creative Expression | Rating: _____

-3          -2          -1          -0          1          2          3

Personal Growth | Rating: _____

-3          -2          -1          -0          1          2          3

Spirituality | Rating: _____

-3          -2          -1          -0          1          2          3

Community Service| Rating: _____

-3          -2          -1          -0          1          2          3

Other: _____ | Rating: _____

| -3 | -2 | -1 | -0 | 1 | 2 | 3 |
|---|---|---|---|---|---|---|

Other: _____ | Rating: _____

| -3 | -2 | -1 | -0 | 1 | 2 | 3 |
|---|---|---|---|---|---|---|

Considering how you've ranked the areas above, pick one area to be your priority for this journey. Keep this in mind as you complete the program.

**My Priority Area for This Journey is** _____

**which I currently rate a** _____ **on a scale of -3 to +3.**

# PERSONAL GROWTH AMBITION CHECK

Using the scale below, mark your agreement with each statement. Then, write your total score in the space below and in the Appendix's Part 1 Log.

1 = Definitely Disagree     2 = Mostly Disagree     3 = Somewhat Disagree

4 = Somewhat Agree     2 = Mostly Agree     3 = Mostly Agree

| Statement | Rating | | | | | |
|---|---|---|---|---|---|---|
| I know how I want my life to be. | 1 | 2 | 3 | 4 | 5 | 6 |
| I know how my life will most likely turn out. | 1 | 2 | 3 | 4 | 5 | 6 |
| I know what my main goals in life are. | 1 | 2 | 3 | 4 | 5 | 6 |
| I have a personal motto, mission, or vision statement. | 1 | 2 | 3 | 4 | 5 | 6 |
| I know which specific things in my life I must change in order to reach my goals. | 1 | 2 | 3 | 4 | 5 | 6 |
| I feel like I can accomplish my main goals for life. | 1 | 2 | 3 | 4 | 5 | 6 |
| I know what my unique contribution to the world around me will be. | 1 | 2 | 3 | 4 | 5 | 6 |
| I have a plan for making my life more balanced. | 1 | 2 | 3 | 4 | 5 | 6 |

**\* Mark the Statement That Draws You the Most.**

TOTAL SCORE _____ [Copy Total To Score Chart in the Appendix]

N.B. If your score 40 - 48, you may not see significant gains from this program.

# PERSONAL STRENGTHS | 30 INGREDIENTS OR TRAITS FOR HAPPINESS AND SUCCESS

1. **Enthusiasm/Interest:**

   eagerness and ardent interest in pursuit of something

2. **Sufficiency/Contentment:**

   having requisite or adequate ability, qualities, and supplies

3. **Hope:**

   desire accompanied by expectation of or belief in fulfillment

4. **Focus:**

   to concentrate attention or effort

5. **Bravery:**

   having or showing mental or moral strength to face

   danger, fear, or difficulty : having or showing

   courage

6. **Realism:**

   the ability to see things as they really

   are and deal with them in a practical way

7. **Solution-Oriented:**

   to actively seek solutions, explanations, or answers for problems.

8. **Durability/Resilience:**

   able to exist for a long time without significant deterioration in quality or value

9. **Authenticity:**

   true to one's own personality, spirit, or character

10. **Organization:**

    having a formal organization or process to coordinate and carry out activities

11. **Picturesque:**

    the presentation of a striking or effective presentation composed of features notable for their distinctness and charm

12. **Gratification:**

    producing pleasure or contentment by providing what is needed or wanted

13. **Rest:**

   having had sufficient rest or sleep

14. **Kindness:**

   choosing to be friendly, generous, and considerate

15. **Support:**

   benefiting from assistance from others, systems, or organizations to

   promote success and minimize consequences of falling short.

16. **Spiritual/Reflective:**

   reflective and seeking on one's conduct, aspirations

17. **Grateful:**

   appreciative of benefits received

18. **Creative:**

   to produce, test or bring about by a course of action or behavior

   some product or effect

19. **Connected:**

   having social, professional, or commercial relationships

20. **Vigorous:**

   carried out forcefully and energetically; full of physical or mental

   strength or active force; assertive

21. **Generous:**

   a willingness and warmhearted readiness to give or provide

   assistance

22. **Graceful:**

   ease and suppleness of movement or bearing that is charming or an

   attractive trait or characteristic

23. **Impressive:**

   having the power to excite attention, awe, or admiration

24. **Impactful:**

   having a noticeable, a significant, or major effect

25. **Memorable:**

being or likely to be noticed especially as being uncommon or extraordinary

26. **Confidence:**

having or showing assurance and self-reliance

27. **Acknowledgment:**

to be publicly recognized, accepted, and/or acknowledged

28. **Intellect:**

to educate oneself through study and training

29. **Thoughtfulness:**

to engage in careful reasoned thinking in anticipation of the needs and wants of yourself and/or others

30. **Nourishment:**

to seek and supply materials and assistance to promote development and improvement for yourself and/or others

# COLOR THERAPY SUMMARY

| CORAL | MAROON | TEAL | COBALT | INDIGO |
|---|---|---|---|---|
| Warmth<br>Acceptance<br>Individuality | Ambition<br>Confidence<br>Acceptance | Morality<br>Renewal<br>Practicality | Ingenuity<br>Solitude<br>Productivity | Integrity<br>Intuition<br>Order |
| **RED**<br>Passion<br>Energy<br>Strength | **ORANGE**<br>Enthusiasm<br>Optimism<br>Youth | **GREEN**<br>Harmony<br>Health<br>Growth | **BLUE**<br>Trust<br>Loyalty<br>Security | **PURPLE**<br>Spirituality<br>Imagination<br>Royalty |
| **LAVENDER**<br>Femininity<br>Tranquility<br>Religion | **COGNAC**<br>Competence<br>Subtlety<br>Affluence | **CHAMPAGNE**<br>Class<br>Modesty<br>Celebration | **TAUPE**<br>Relaxation<br>Contentment<br>Neutrality | **BRONZE**<br>Strength<br>Support<br>Loyalty |
| **PINK**<br>Compassion<br>Love<br>Playfulness | **BROWN**<br>Stability<br>Honesty<br>Comfort | **YELLOW**<br>Happiness<br>Positivity<br>Intellect | **TURQUOISE**<br>Calmness<br>Clarity<br>Compassion | **MAGENTA**<br>Kindness<br>Character<br>Change |
| **LILAC**<br>Helpfulness<br>Serenity<br>Kindness | **GOLD**<br>Wealth<br>Success<br>Prestige | **BEIGE**<br>Simplicity<br>Tranquility<br>Modernism | **VIOLET**<br>Wisdom<br>Sensitivity<br>Creativity | **AMBER**<br>Joy<br>Positivity<br>Energy |
| **WHITE**<br>Purity<br>Innocence<br>Cleanliness | **SILVER**<br>Affluence<br>Intuition<br>Illumination | **GREY**<br>Compromise<br>Neutrality<br>Practicality | **SEAFOAM**<br>Revitalization<br>Luck<br>Health | **BLACK**<br>Power<br>Protection<br>Elegance |

| Day | Flow Verse | Success Ingredient | Activity | Color Therapy | Tarot |
|-----|------------|--------------------|---------|----------------|-------|
| 1 | Empathy for the Young Queen | Enthusiasm | 3 Paths to Happiness | Orange | The Fool |
| 2 | The Last Time | Sufficiency/ Contentment | Personal Strength Assessment | Teal | The Magician |
| 3 | A Glimpse of the Unknown | Hope | Guiding Stars | Beige | The High Priestess |
| 4 | Regret | Focus | Personal Mission Statement | Cognac | The Empress |
| 5 | The Beast Within | Bravery | iSMARTER Goals & Contract | Red | The Emperor |
| 6 | Arise! | Realism | Obstacles & Emotional Triggers | Bronze | The Hierophant |

| Day | Flow Verse | Success Ingredient | Activity | Color Therapy | Tarot |
|---|---|---|---|---|---|
| 7 | Danger | Solution-Oriented | Solution Framework | Indigo | The Lovers |
| 8 | Bring It | Durable | Daily Routine Review | Taupe | The Chariot |
| 9 | Confrontation | Authentic | Safety Crutches | Black | Justice |
| 10 | The Devil - Reversed | Organized | Plan of Attack | Turquoise | The Hermit |
| 11 | Power Trip | Picturesque | Improving Spaces | Grey | Wheel of Fortune |
| 12 | Black Queen Magic | Gratified | Self-Love Quiz | Champagne | Strength |

| Day | Flow Verse | Success Ingredient | Activity | Color Therapy | Tarot |
|---|---|---|---|---|---|
| 13 | Motivation | Rested | Self-Care Rituals | Gold | The *Dead* Man |
| 14 | Victory for the Weary | Kindness | Compli-ments | Violet | Death |
| 15 | I've Been Changed - Verse 3 | Supported | Emotional Toolkit & Midpoint Reflection | Brown | Temperance |
| 16 | I've Been Changed - Verse 4 | Spiritual | Loving-Kindness | Coral | The Devil |
| 17 | Is This What You Want? | Grateful | Gratitude Practices | Silver | The Tower |
| 18 | Real Talk | Creative | Brainstorming | Lavender | The Star |

| Day | Flow Verse | Success Ingredient | Activity | Color Therapy | Tarot |
|---|---|---|---|---|---|
| 19 | Celebrity | Connected | Managing Support Systems | Amber | The Moon |
| 20 | I've Been Changed - Verse 5 | Vigorous | Stress | Cobalt | The Sun |
| 21 | Making It | Generous | Listening Skills | Magenta | Judgement |
| 22 | Don't Blow It | Graceful | Pro-Social Spending | Green | The World |
| 23 | I Know I've Been Changed - Verse 1 | Impressive | 360° Self | Yellow | Eight of Cups |
| 24 | Dropped | Impactful | Managing Perspectives | Lilac | Ace of Pentacles |

| Day | Flow Verse | Success Ingredient | Activity | Color Therapy | Tarot |
|-----|-----------|--------------------|----------|---------------|-------|
| 25 | I've Been Changed - Verse 6 | Memorable | PR Campaign | Marron | Life Summary |
| 26 | Consort | Confidence | Boundaries | Pink | Empathic Reappraisal |
| 27 | Decay | Acknowledg-ment | Imagined Conversations | Magenta | Overcoming Vices |
| 28 | You Don't Get It | Intellect | Therapeutic Homework | Sea-foam | Environment Assessment |
| 29 | Forbidden Fruit | Thoughtful-ness | Automatic Thoughts | White | Affirmation Toolkit |
| 30 | Secret Sauce | Nourishment | Self-Soothing | Purple | Diva Meditation |

**MONTH/YEAR:** _____

| SUN | MON | TUE | WED | THU | FRI | SAT |
|-----|-----|-----|-----|-----|-----|-----|
|  |  |  |  |  |  |  |
|  |  |  |  |  |  |  |
|  |  |  |  |  |  |  |
|  |  |  |  |  |  |  |
|  |  |  |  |  |  |  |
|  |  |  |  |  |  |  |

**PRIORITIES**

☐ _____

☐ _____

☐ _____

☐ _____

**NOTES** _____

_____

_____

_____

_____

Blank Page

**MONTH/YEAR:** _____

| SUN | MON | TUE | WED | THU | FRI | SAT |
|-----|-----|-----|-----|-----|-----|-----|
|     |     |     |     |     |     |     |
|     |     |     |     |     |     |     |
|     |     |     |     |     |     |     |
|     |     |     |     |     |     |     |
|     |     |     |     |     |     |     |
|     |     |     |     |     |     |     |

**PRIORITIES**

☐ _____

☐ _____

☐ _____

☐ _____

**NOTES** _____

_____

_____

_____

_____

Blank Page

# ABOUT MY MOOD TRACKER METHOD

A useful method for tracking your progress is to use a mood tracker. I like this design since it allows you to be creative. However, to you'll need to commit to a consistent design for the whole program or at least each 6-day period. You can either take a day off each week or complete the petals each day for 30 days. There's a blank template in the appendix for you to make copies as needed.

## MOOD TRACKER: COMMITMENT SCHEDULE

I commit to recording my mood at these times:

Morning: _____ a.m.

Midday: _____ a.m /p.m.

Evening: _____ p.m.

_____
Signature

Copyright © 2022 by Naci Sigler
All Rights Reserved.

COLOR PETAL ON

MOOD TRACKER - MORNING

READ DAILY FLOW

COMPLETE REFLECTION 1

COMPLETE DAILY ACTIVITY

COMPLETE DAILY REVIEW

COLOR PETAL ON

MOOD TRACKER - AFTERNOON

COLOR PETAL ON

MOOD TRACKER - EVENING

## Week of:

**NOTES**

### Days 1 - 6: Morning Mood Tracker

Blank Page

Blank Page

Blank Page

# DAY ONE

## Flow | Empathy for the Young Queen

Before me stands a young queen

Amidst turmoil, I too have lived and seen

It tears me apart to see you in such pain

I too hate there's a cost for every gain.

For riches are both a blessing and a burdensome tether,

This too will get somewhat easier,

but not necessarily fully resolved or better.

What has your personal growth "cost" you? What have you had to let go or feel you missed out on?

_____

_____

_____

What is a primary source of your turmoil?

_____

_____

_____

How do you think that issue will be resolved ultimately?

_____

_____

# Quiz | What's Your General Enthusiasm Level

**Check the boxes next to the statement that are generally true for you.**

Do you feel as though you lack purpose or don't contribute enough to society/those around you?

Are you disinterested in recognition, achievement, and success?

Do you feel that your life has been mostly a series of failures and disappointments?

Are you depressed? Have you noticed a significant decrease concern, interest, or emotion about anything?

Do you have a chronic illness or terminal illness?

Is substance abuse an issue for you?

Do you feel a discouraging sense of powerlessness in your daily life?

Do you exhibit a general lack of respect for others like deliberately ignoring others?

Are you late or fail showing up at all to important meetings, appointments, or events?

Is it rare for you to get excited by something?

*If you checked 2 or more of the above, you may have a noticeable lack of enthusiasm for life.*

**Date:** _____

## TODAY'S STRENGTH FOCUS

_____

### GOLD STAR MOMENT

_____
_____
_____

### DIFFICULT MOMENT

_____
_____
_____

### SOMETHING THAT HELPED

_____
_____
_____

### HOW I COULD HAVE RESPONDED

_____
_____
_____

### STRENGTH FOCUS POTENTIAL USES

**PERSONAL LIFE**

**WORK LIFE**

**FAMILY & FRIENDS**

**RELATIONSHIP**

**NOTES**

_____
_____
_____

# Business Day-Time Schedule

| Time & Activity | Notes |
|---|---|
| 8:00 | |
| 8:30 | |
| 9:00 | |
| 9:30 | |
| 10:00 | |
| 10:30 | |
| 11:00 | |
| 11:30 | |
| 12:00 | |
| 12:30 | |
| 1:00 | |
| 1:30 | |
| 2:00 | |
| 2:30 | |
| 3:00 | |
| 3:30 | |
| 4:00 | |
| 4:30 | |
| 5:00 | |

# ENTHUSIASM

> Success consists of going from failure to failure without loss of enthusiasm.
>
> - Winston Churchill

**Enthusiasm** is particularly a happy trait and a vital part of all three routes to happiness! Its key characteristics are interest, enthusiasm, and positivity. It encourages us to seek out and savor life's moments. How will you do that today?

## ASSOCIATED WORDS

- Enthusiastic - Vigorous -
- Energetic - Perky - Peppy -

## WHAT SORT OF ACTIVITIES FILL YOU WITH ENERGY?

_____

_____

_____

_____

### ORANGE

**SYMBOLIZES**

Emotion
Youth
Enthusiasm

**EFFECTS**

Encourages
Uplifts
Excites

**POSITIVES**

Spontaneity
Creativity
Liveliness

**NEGATIVES**

Unreliable
Immature
Unstable

Blank Page

A negative event that made a strong impression on me was....

In other words, it made me feel like I was...

_____

[negative word]

In hindsight, this benefited me because...

Success/Happiness Ingredients that I'd use if I were placed in this situation again are...

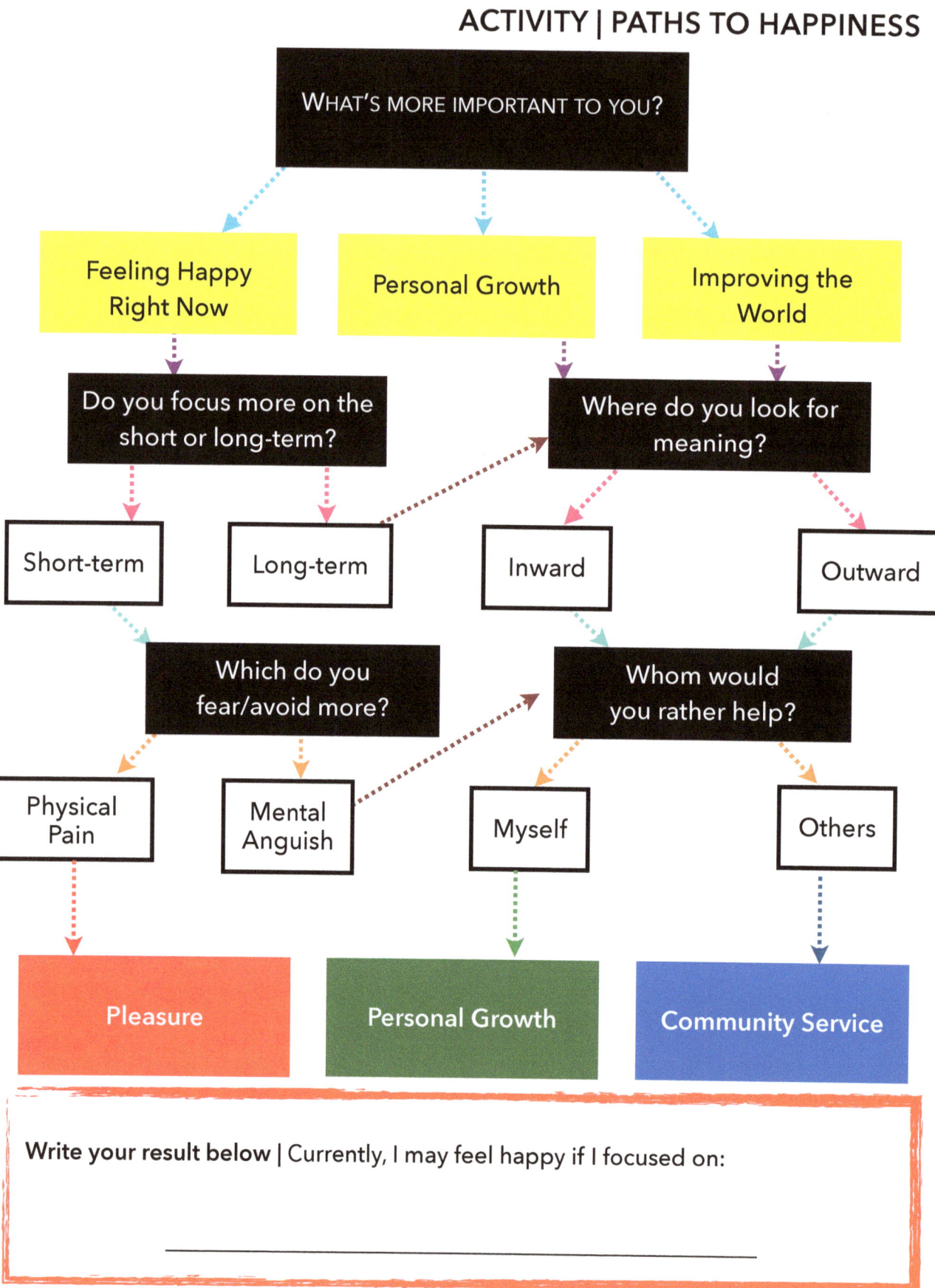

**Write your result below** | Currently, I may feel happy if I focused on:

_____

### The Pleasure Path

If your quiz indicates that you may be happiness focusing on your own pleasure, this means that you're inclined to avoid "pain" at this point. On this path, an important consideration is that this pursuit could lead to unhealthy behaviors and pursuits. For instance, if you are focused on short-term pleasures, you may be more inclined to indulge yourself. This could make it more difficult for you to accomplish your goals. Alternatively, if you tend to feel as though you have or had to deny yourself, this could also be a reaction to that. There's nothing inherently wrong with the pursuit of pleasure, as long as you're conscious that it's also vital to do so responsibly.

### Personal Growth

The inclination to focus on your personal growth means that you wish to or are currently actively pursuing opportunities to improve yourself. On this path, a key consideration is whether this prompts you to be overly egocentric. In other words, this may make you more likely to dismiss other pursuits that you believe or feel aren't compatible with your chosen path. Accordingly, you could miss out on opportunities to broaden your horizons. On the other hand, this could also indicate that you are simply committed to achieving your goals or maintaining a healthier lifestyle.

## Community Service

If you are or wish to prioritize community service, this indicates that you are inclined to take a larger perspective or longer-term view on how your actions impact others and the environment. For example, you could be a more family-oriented person or have been/are significantly influenced by a culture promoting this mindset. This doesn't mean that you reject or are not concerned with things that do not promote this. It may simply indicate that you are more focused on making a meaningful contribution to the community.

## SELF-DEVELOPMENT & LEARNING

## RELATIONSHIPS

## CAREER & FINANCES

## HEALTH & WELLNESS

**PATH TO HAPPINESS | Who or What Am I Called to Be?**

Review what you wrote for this activity previously. Considering what your path to happiness results, how do you think you should be in each area now?

## ABOUT THE CARD

The serpent pictured refers to the Judeo-Christian depiction of Satan as a snake that successfully tempted Eden to go against God. Ultimately, there was little gain for Satan other than his pleasure in damaging God's relationship with his children with bad, everlasting consequences for himself.

**REVERSED: Immaturity - Carelessness - Distraction - Foolishness**

The fool does not maturely plan his path. He exists merely for the entertainment of others. Living a life overly focused on others could deprive you of the meaningful opportunity to enjoy fulfilling personal growth. Be mindful of the possible dangers that lie on your path. The fool's simple existence in service of others also symbolizes an inherent childishness. He refuses to take responsibility for himself and relies on those around him to act responsibly.

**UPRIGHT: New Beginnings - Freedom - Openness - Bravery - Hope**

But, the fool is not wholly negative. For example, while the fool's immaturity is a serious character flaw, there are good things associated with that sort of youthful outlook. In fact, children can be remarkably brave and persistent. It takes a lot of spirit and determination to learn vital skills like walking. You are literally constantly faced with being frustrated by your limitations and lack of progress compared to others around you. However, since children have all their needs met, they are free of the daily burdens that adults are required to face and navigate. So, they have the opportunity to enjoy a less-stressful existence and are free to focus on whatever interests them. Assuming that the adults responsible for them have the means to care for them well.

## ACTIVATING THE FOOL'S POWER

Naturally, we all have both these positive and negative aspects ourselves. So, while the fool symbolizes a powerful warning, he also inspires courage. He unquestionably accepts the riskiness that always surrounds us. He's unashamed of his perceived ignorance. Indeed, comedy is a powerful force capable of defusing tension and facilitating humanity's unity through shared laughter. The Fool exists to serve royalty and is always present among them. This means that he has a uniquely powerful position to observe the inner workings of power and perhaps even subtly influence them with a particularly cutting remark.

Thus, the Fool - like all other cards in the tarot deck - has an inherent **duality**. As is the case with our flawed humanity, this means that this card has both positive and negative associations.

Activate your ability to accept that there's always a duality present in our life circumstances (i.e. both good and bad). Commit yourself to writing down your thoughts as you consider bothersome or risky situations. This step is vital to confronting the reality of your situation. If you're unable or unwilling to actually fully face something, you aren't demonstrating the maturity and honesty required of a queen. How can you rule your empire if you'd rather play the fool? Either own your flaws or relinquish the crown.

## ACTIONS AND CONSIDERATIONS FOR DRAWING THIS CARD

Think carefully about something that's really been bothering you.

**How should you maturely think about and plans for the problems caused by that?**

The fool also encourages us to be brave and to recognize the benefits associated with our current situation. So, you should next think about how your current circumstances benefit you.

**How does dealing with this situation relate positively to your personal growth journey?**

Blank Page

## - A WARNING AND AN OPPORTUNITY -

I'll get no rest
From the obstacles to my success.
You see to compete,
you must accept that victory comes only after
many struggles and countless defeats.

| UPRIGHT | REVERSED |
|---|---|
| New Beginnings, | Immaturity; |
| Freedom; | Carelessness; |
| Openness; | Distraction; |
| Bravery, Hope | Foolishness |

*"The price of greatness is responsibility."*
- Winston Churchill

## – THE FOOL –

Blank Page

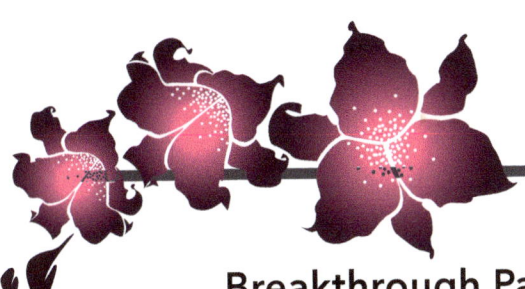

# Breakthrough Path Finder - Activating the Fool's Power

1. What problem/issue is the focus?

_____

_____

_____

2. What's the worst case scenario for you personally? If you asked the other people involved, would they agree with this? If not, what do you think they'd rather be emphasized?

_____

_____

_____

3. Does this situation really have the ability to powerfully impact you in a wholly negative way overall? If not, then why are you allowing it to bother you?

_____

_____

_____

4. If the situation is crucial, are you taking it enough?

_____

_____

_____

5. What would be your ideal solution vs. what could you ultimately learn to accept?

_____

_____

_____

6. What concrete steps should you actively and intentionally be making in order to make the situation at least tolerable?

_____

_____

_____

7. Are you unwilling to accept anything that isn't mostly your ideal solution? If the answer is yes, would it be better for you to plan to exit the situation? If you're unwilling to compromise or leave, what does that say about you? Are you okay with that?

_____

_____

_____

_____

# DAY TWO

## THE LAST TIME

You came at me sidewise - wild and unstrung.

I let you vent - I held my tongue.

Pure ignorance - do what you will…

I sat in silence - held my piece still

I let you finish the rant you'd begun

I looked at you coldly - then said "I'm done".

How do you handle upset people? Do you let them vent or cut them off?

_____

_____

_____

What behavior do you simply refuse to accept?

_____

_____

_____

Is there a role model that you'd like to emulate when it comes to handling confrontation?

_____

_____

# DAY 2 REVIEW & PLAN

**Date:** _____

## YESTERDAY'S STRENGTH FOCUS

_____

### GOLD STAR MOMENT

_____

_____

_____

### DIFFICULT MOMENT

_____

_____

_____

### SOMETHING THAT HELPED

_____

_____

_____

### HOW I COULD HAVE RESPONDED

_____

_____

## TODAY'S STRENGTH FOCUS

_____

### STRENGTH FOCUS POTENTIAL USES

**PERSONAL LIFE**

**WORK LIFE**

**FAMILY & FRIENDS**

**RELATIONSHIP**

**NOTES**

_____

_____

_____

# Business Day-Time Schedule

| Time & Activity | | Notes |
|---|---|---|
| 8:00 | | |
| 8:30 | | |
| 9:00 | | |
| 9:30 | | |
| 10:00 | | |
| 10:30 | | |
| 11:00 | | |
| 11:30 | | |
| 12:00 | | |
| 12:30 | | |
| 1:00 | | |
| 1:30 | | |
| 2:00 | | |
| 2:30 | | |
| 3:00 | | |
| 3:30 | | |
| 4:00 | | |
| 4:30 | | |
| 5:00 | | |

A negative event that made a strong impression on me was....

In other words, it made me feel like I was...

_____
[negative word]

In hindsight, this benefited me because...

Success/Happiness Ingredients that I'd use if I were placed in this situation again are...

# QUIZ | ARE YOU GENERALLY SATISFIED WITH YOUR LIFE?

**Check the boxes next to the statement that are generally true for you.**

| | |
|---|---|
| Do you feel unhappy with your life overall? | |
| Is it difficult for you to feel relaxed? | |
| Do you frequently find yourself comparing your life to others? | |
| Are you depressed? Have you noticed a significant decrease concern, interest, or emotion about anything? | |
| If your life were to end in the next few minutes, would you be happy with the life you've led? | |
| Do you have enough to meet your basic needs? | |
| Do you feel that you are frequently being harassed, discriminated against, and/or used? | |
| Are you frequently worried about money or being unable to take care of yourself or your responsibilities? | |
| Do you feel unsafe in your regular surroundings? | |
| Do you feel like a disappointment? | |

*If you checked 3 or more of the above, you may be significantly unhappy with your life.*

# CONTENTMENT

"Many people lose the small joys in the hope for the big happiness."
— Pearl S. Buck

**Contentment** is a vital ingredient since it allows us to identify the sources and status of things that make us happy and successful. It encourages us to remedy issues and enjoy our happiness/success. What issue do you need to tackle today?

## ASSOCIATED WORDS

Renewal, Earnestness, Objectivity, Morality

## WHAT PLACES/ACTIVITIES MAKE YOU RELAXED AND HAPPY?

_____

_____

_____

_____

## TEAL

**SYMBOLIZES**

Renewal
Vigilance
Objectivity

**EFFECTS**

Enlightens
Supports
Inspires

**POSITIVES**

Openness
Rationality
Supportive

**NEGATIVES**

Controlling
Suspicious
Standoffish

Blank Page

Re-read the 30 Ingredients for Happiness and Success in the book's forward.

Then, complete the activities below.

## WHICH 5 TRAITS DO YOU BELIEVE MANY PEOPLE WOULD ASSOCIATE WITH YOU?

| | | | | |
|---|---|---|---|---|
| Enthusiasm / Interest | Sufficency/ Contentment | Hope | Focus | Bravery |
| Realistic | Solution-Oriented | Durable | Authentic | Orangized |
| Picturesque | Gratified | Rested | Hearty | Supported |
| Spiritual/ Reflective | Grateful | Creative | Connected | Vigorous |
| Generous | Impressive | Confidence | Recognized/ Acknowledged | Intellectual |
| Memorable | Thoughtful | Nourishing | Impressive | Impactful |

# WHICH 5 TRAITS DO THE PEOPLE YOU ADMIRE HAVE?

| | | | | |
|---|---|---|---|---|
| Enthusiasm / Interest | Sufficency/ Contentment | Hope | Focus | Bravery |
| Realistic | Solution-Oriented | Durable | Authentic | Orangized |
| Picturesque | Gratified | Rested | Hearty | Supported |
| Spiritual/ Reflective | Grateful | Creative | Connected | Vigorous |
| Generous | Impressive | Confidence | Recognized/ Acknowledged | Intellectual |
| Memorable | Thoughtful | Nourishing | Impressive | Impactful |

# WHICH 5 TRAITS DO YOU WANT ASSOCIATED WITH YOU?

| | | | | |
|---|---|---|---|---|
| Enthusiasm / Interest | Sufficency/ Contentment | Hope | Focus | Bravery |
| Realistic | Solution-Oriented | Durable/ Resilient | Authentic | Orangized |
| Picturesque | Gratified | Rested | Hearty | Supported |
| Spiritual/ Reflective | Grateful | Creative | Connected | Vigorous |
| Generous | Impressive | Confidence | Recognized/ Acknowledged | Intellectual |
| Memorable | Thoughtful | Nourishing | Impressive | Impactful |

## About the Card

In essence, the Magician card represents all possibilities, creation, and willpower. Be mindful, however, since the magician's creative potential may also be used to create convincing illusions! It symbolizes the connection between higher consciousness/God and our reality, all four elements - air, earth, fire, and water, and all cards in the tarot deck.

## REVERSED:

This card reverses cautions you to act with care! A skilled magician excites and draws us in with convincing illusion and deception. So, there may be someone or some force manipulating you. Carefully consider how the motivations and concerns of other players differ from your own. How might they gain at your expense?

Another crucial element to consider is how you may also be unconsciously using your power to deceive yourself. Are your actions or inaction creating conditions that are not in your favor? Consider your present state of self. Or, perhaps you may be deluding yourself to believe that some sort of development or showy/conspicuous effort is genuine? Remember that things are not always as they seem…

## UPRIGHT:

Drawing an upright magician means that you should seriously consider embracing opportunity and/or taking action without hesitation. It signifies the alignment of your whole self, positive possibilities, and other conditions of the universe. Now's the time for you to actively work toward manifesting your desires. First, satisfy yourself that no apparent deception or illusions on your part. Gather your courage and resources, and go for it!

## Activating the Magician's Power

Activate your ability to accept that there's always a duality present in our life circumstances (i.e. both good and bad). Commit yourself to writing down your thoughts as you consider bothersome or risky situations. This step is vital to confronting the reality of your situation. If you're unable or unwilling to actually fully face something, you aren't demonstrating the maturity and honesty required of a queen. How can you rule your empire if you'd rather play the fool? Either own your flaws or relinquish the crown.

This card is all about your inherent power, my queen. As a deciding factor in your own and the lives of others, it is vital that you carefully consider the environment before undertaking/authorizing deliberate action. Now's the time for you to pause and mindfully journal. If you make any miscalculations, you'll need to understand what your thought process was so that you do not repeat your mistakes. Be sure to record the following:

1. Summarize your understanding and feelings toward of the situation as a whole.

2. List all the relevant players, your resources and the current environmental factors. It may be useful to consider your dilemma as a map or board. Mark your position and the path forward. Where do you anticipate obstacles? What are the other potential pathways you could take or switch to if necessary? You are actively brainstorming here and producing the first draft of your plan of action.

3. Now, decide how long you have before you need to make a decision. Take that into consideration and build in some time for you to set this aside. Schedule the time when you'll revisit this. You should allow your unconscious mind time to reflect on your understanding and receive other signs from the universe. Tend to other matters and increase your self-care

activities. You need to be rested, prepared, and clear-headed before moving forward.

4. Retrieve your first draft. Before reviewing it, write down your intention/goal. Then, review your plan/map and make any changes in a different color pen/pencil. Afterwards, neatly re-write it. Are you feeling confident that this is currently your best strategy moving forward? If not, why? Use another page to note any hesitations/concerns that you have. Are you able to favorably influence any of these before you act? If not, mindfully imbue these much positive intention and allow yourself to release them.

## Actions and Considerations for Drawing This Card

Take a minute and mindfully pause. First, ask yourself…

**Am I missing something?**

Then, grab some paper or your journal, it's time to strategize!

**What are my intentions or hopes here? What's my best path forward?**

Blank Page

**- CONNECTING HEAVEN AND EARTH -**
**- INFINITE POSSIBILITIES -**

I have the faith, hope, and belief
To embrace my possibilities & foresee potential
defeat.
Grant me guidance and insight too
For I have much consideration to do....

**UPRIGHT**                           **REVERSED**

Infinite Possibility                          Illusion

Manifestation                             Deception

Willpower                                  Caution

*"We must accept finite disappointment, but*
*never lose infinite hope."*

- Martin Luther King, Jr.

# – THE MAGICIAN –

Blank Page

# DAY THREE

## FLOW | A GLIMPSE OF THE UNKNOWN

You asked for guidance and inspiration

To help you see the warnings and other indications.

But, now you feel your hesitation…

To confront the reality of your situation.

You can stay and tolerate the stagnation

Or you can move on to your next destination.

So, do you choose preservation?

Or are you brave enough to chase transformation?

How do you seek guidance and inspiration (e.g. discussions with others, meditation, prayer)?

_____

_____

_____

What are you hesitant to face? Do you believe that you are capable of triumphing over it?

_____

_____

_____

Do you choose preservation or transformation?

_____

_____

# DAY 3 | REVIEW AND PLAN

**Date:** _____

## YESTERDAY'S STRENGTH FOCUS

_____

### GOLD STAR MOMENT

_____

_____

_____

### DIFFICULT MOMENT

_____

_____

_____

### SOMETHING THAT HELPED

_____

_____

### HOW I COULD HAVE RESPONDED

_____

_____

## TODAY'S STRENGTH FOCUS

_____

### STRENGTH FOCUS POTENTIAL USES

**PERSONAL LIFE**

**WORK LIFE**

**FAMILY & FRIENDS**

**RELATIONSHIP**

**NOTES**

_____

_____

_____

# Business Day-Time Schedule

| Time & Activity | | Notes |
|---|---|---|
| **8:00** | | |
| **8:30** | | |
| **9:00** | | |
| **9:30** | | |
| **10:00** | | |
| **10:30** | | |
| **11:00** | | |
| **11:30** | | |
| **12:00** | | |
| **12:30** | | |
| **1:00** | | |
| **1:30** | | |
| **2:00** | | |
| **2:30** | | |
| **3:00** | | |
| **3:30** | | |
| **4:00** | | |
| **4:30** | | |
| **5:00** | | |

# Another Take...
## Reflect | Embrace | Grow

A negative event that made a strong impression on me was....




In other words, it made me feel like I was...

_____
[negative word]

In hindsight, this benefited me because...


Success/Happiness Ingredients that I'd use if I were placed in this situation again are...

# HOPE

**Hope** is a vital ingredient since it promotes positive feelings like optimism. It allows us to be brave & envision potential sources of wellbeing and successful. What's your biggest hope for today? How can you make progress toward that?

## BEIGE

**ASSOCIATED WORDS**

Simplicity, Conformity, Comfort

**YOU PERSONALLY ASSOCIATE THE COLOR BEIGE WITH...**

_____

_____

_____

_____

_____

**SYMBOLIZES**

Warmth
Simplicity
Conformity

**EFFECTS**

Soothes
Unifies
Simplifies

**POSITIVES**

Welcoming
Safe
Encouraging

**NEGATIVES**

Boring
Basic
Standardized

Blank Page

Step 1: Choose 3 traits you want associated with you to be your Guiding Stars. Write them in the spaces below. Then, turn back to your pre-journey personal growth ambition. Does it fit with your Guiding Stars? If not, choose a new one. See an example below.

IMPRESSIVE

VIGOROUS

PICTURESQUE

**CURRENT PERSONAL GROWTH AMBITION**

TO KNOW WHAT MY UNIQUE

CONTRIBUTION TO THE WORLD MIGHT BE

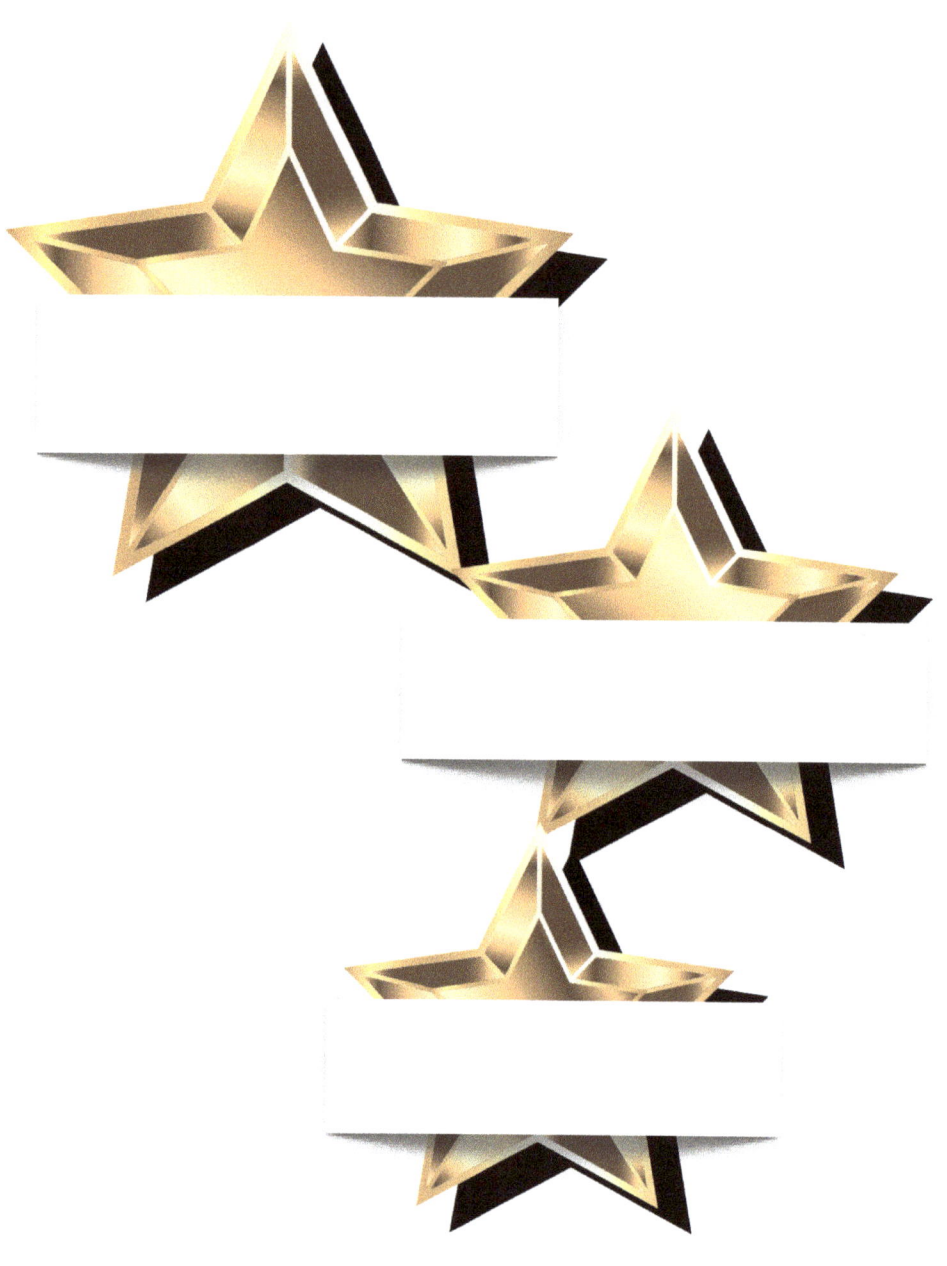

## CURRENT PERSONAL GROWTH AMBITION

_____

_____

A behavior change that I'd really like to see in myself is...

What I really hope happens when I reach my goals is...

My Hopes & Dreams

This would make my present daily life more in line with my goals. Specifically, I already know that this would be different...

www.ingramcontent.com/pod-product-compliance
Lightning Source LLC
Chambersburg PA
CBHW041516120626
46551CB00018B/2461